# PAULUS OF TARSUS
## A Man Driven by the Word

*Presenters: Saint Paul, Lord Jesus/Yeshua, Jose Barnabas, Saint Peter, Saint Luke*

*Verling CHAKO Priest, PhD*

Cover layout by Author and Trafford Publishing.

The painting of Saint Paul is by Michelangelo and the patent and license on it has expired so it is freely given to the public.

Order this book online at www.trafford.com
or email orders@trafford.com

Most Trafford titles are also available at major online book retailers.

Printed in the United States of America.

ISBN: 978-1-4669-2091-0 (sc)
ISBN: 978-1-4669-2090-3 (e)

Trafford rev. 03/14/2012

 www.trafford.com

North America & international
toll-free: 1 888 232 4444 (USA & Canada)
phone: 250 383 6864 ♦ fax: 812 355 4082

# LIST OF BOOKS

The Ultimate Experience, the Many Paths to God series:

BOOKS 1, 2, & 3, REVISITED (2011)

ISBN# 978-1-4269-7664-3

REALITIES of the CRUCIFIXION (2006)

ISBN # 1-4251-0716-8

MESSAGES from the HEAVENLY HOSTS (2007)
ISBN # 1-4251-2550-6

YOUR SPACE BROTHERS and SISTERS GREET YOU!
(2008)

ISBN # 978-1-4251-6302-0

TEACHINGS of the MASTERS of LIGHT (2008)

ISBN # 978-1-4251-8573-2

THE GODDESS RETURNS TO EARTH (2010)

ISBN # 978-1-4269-3563-3

Available at Trafford: 1-888-232-4444

Or, Amazon.com

www.godumentary.com/chako.htm

# DEDICATION

*And it came to pass, that as I made my journey, and was come nigh unto Damascus about noon, suddenly there shone from Heaven a great Light round me. (Acts 22:6)*

*And I fell unto the ground, and heard a voice saying unto me, Saul, Saul, why persecutest thou me? (7)*

*And when I could not see for the glory of that Light, being led by the hand of them that were with me, I came into Damascus. (11)*

*(An-a-ni-as) Came unto me, and stood and said, Brother Saul, receive thy sight. (13)*

*And he said, The God of our fathers hath chosen thee, that thou shouldest know his will, and see that Just One, and shouldest hear the voice of his mouth. (14)*

***For thou shalt be his witness unto all men of what thou hast seen and heard. (15)***

*(Thus Christianity transmigrated unto the Gentiles through the Apostle Paul.)*

# ACKNOWLEDGMENTS

Of course my first Acknowledgment must be to the Lord Jesus the Christ/Yeshua. I thank Him from the bottom of my heart. He would come right in and set me back on track with His beautiful chapters for this book. Thank you beloved brother.

Heather Clarke agreed to take me on for another editing assignment on my book. She is such a part of my book-writing equation; I do not know how I could venture forth without her! Heather is founder of the *Arizona Enlightenment Center* and hence has her fingers on the spiritual pulse of the Valley. Therefore, I greatly appreciate the time and energy she so cheerfully gives to me whenever I am in a book-writing mode. Hugs to you, dear friend.

My daughter, Susan O'Brien, is my computer help-mate. She cheerfully takes all of my book-files and frames them into book-form. She is the one who found the cover painting for me that held no license or patent—they had expired and the painting was now free for the public's use. So thank you once again, my dearest heart of hearts.

Readers, I give you my grateful thanks for participating in purchasing and reading of my many books. We speak to you often throughout these pages—always striving for clarification for you. We thank you for your willingness to look at new belief systems and perhaps make changes with your own. Blessings, Chako.

(*And let us not be weary in well doing: for in due season we shall reap, if we faint not. Ga. 6:9*)

# PREFACE

Dear Readers, I have heard from many of you, wanting to know when my next book would be published. I have spent most of 2009 having two knee joint replacements and recovering from those operations. I could only focus on healing and not on writing a book.

Yeshua was with me every step of the way, even cleansing the blood of a transfusion through His filters before it entered my body. (I was concerned about taking on the donor's karma through his/her blood.)

I recently spoke with Yeshua through the voice channel, Cynthia Williams. I voiced my concerns to Him about returning to my telepathic channeling after such a long sabbatical. He told me that I was attempting to channel in the previous way, and it was no longer viable for me. I was to find a new way to bring in a book. I asked Him if He would still come to me. He assured me that He would but to keep in mind that He wears a coat of many colors. (*Would I always recognize that it is He?*)

Therefore, the next day I entered into meditation, wondering if anyone would come to speak to me. Shortly thereafter I heard, *Good day to you; peace be with you.* I knew it was Yeshua. He introduced Himself and then told me that my next book would not be orchestrated by Him; that He would no longer hold our little conversations before and after a Presenter. He offered that He would be happy to give me a paragraph or a chapter for the book if I wished. He said that the previous five published books were part of a series, and that that series had been completed. It was now time for me to create something different.

I thought that the only way to break away from the previous mold was to completely redesign the book cover and change the format in the book itself. That is why you will notice several changes. Also I decided to start the book from the beginning grammatically in the first person—to channel Saint Paul/Paulus/Saul and to see where he would lead me, 10-29-09 & 3-09-12.

Readers, I always have let my process of writing a book be open and truthful for you. I let you see my gaffs, and my struggles with the channeling at times. This book did not flow from cover to cover. It had starts and stops, fits and sighs, and at times I questioned what I had gotten myself into! I began yelling to Yeshua to come grab the tiller of this boat.

He came with His usual peace and humor and smoothed over my ruffled feathers as He brought the Presenters forth for me. (It seemed as if when I sat to bring them forth, there was just ensuing silence. As soon as Yeshua showed up, the channeling flowed once again.)

Well, I was sailing along, I thought, when Yeshua came in and started dictation for the book. Half way through, He calmly stated that this segment would be the *Closing Statement*! "Holy Cow," I muttered to myself, the book only had about 70+ pages. This is not going to be a book, per se, but a book-**let**! Boy, when He takes the helm of your boat, be prepared, for you may be docked before your known ETA (*estimated time of arrival*).

Now you know, Readers, I can't play victim here. I obviously on some level had agreed to this abrupt ending. It may have been as simple as "enough already!" The purpose of the book was to bring a new perspective about Saint Paul's life. I think we have succeeded extraordinarily. So get into your comfy chair, put your feet up, and have a glass of good clean water nearby and get ready to have all of your preconceived ideas about our Paulus refuted, reshuffled, and transmuted!

*(When I was a child, I spake as a child, I understood as a child, I thought as a child: but when I became a man, I put away childish things. 1Co 13:11).*

*I had a small gathering of 16 people at my home Sunday, October 25, 2009, from 2:00 to 4:00. Cynthia Williams, a voice channel, had brought forth Yeshua ben Joseph/ Jesus for his monthly teachings. Half way through his message, the front door of my house flew open. Yeshua greeted the soul, and we all laughed for we saw no one. The door was then shut and locked this time and the class continued. Afterwards, Cynthia said the "visitor" was a beautiful, benevolent soul who was drawn to the Light she perceived as she walked by my house. Since the house was filled with Yeshua and the many Lightworkers' Lights, the soul felt drawn to come in. When Yeshua had finished His teachings and withdrew from Cynthia's body and the group, He took the soul-visitor with Him and no doubt returned her to her body. That was a lesson for all of us—different souls can enter into homes and bodies without our knowing, for they are always drawn to the energy with which they resonate—Light or shadow.

# PROLOGUE

**I AM Saul of Tarsus, or Paulus**, using my Roman name. I will not add *Saint* before my name, for I feel that the many noble Saints that grace Heaven are more deserving of that title than I, perhaps. During the time that I walked the Earth, I pontificated what I thought were the teachings of Jesus/Yeshua, and I was not conscious of the future repercussions if my interpretations were incorrect in any way. (*Channeled by Chako.*)

I, Paul, was molding Yeshua's words into a religion that would be known as *Christianity,* with the worshippers being known as the *Body of Christ.* This concept was against everything that Yeshua had taught, I now realize. He abhorred the idea that people must sit in a *box (church)* and be taught dogma. He abhorred being given God status versus being known as an example of how Man could raise himself up from the depths of lower humanity. The Kingdom of God needs to be reached via the heart and not through a priest whose level of consciousness could be at a lower level than your own!

Hence, a religion was born—a distorted adaptation of what Yeshua was teaching—distributed by an over-zealous mind that was disconnected from its own heart—mine. Thus this book is my attempt at redemption! Let me go back and bring truth and love into my narration, and not pride in my passion for spreading to the Jews and Gentiles what I thought were His Words and the meaning of the Kingdom of God.

I was a Jew from the tribe of Benjamin, raised in the strict tradition of the Pharisees. Law ruled my father's house.* Love was a concept that was correlated strongly with duty—duty to Law, duty to one's parents, and duty to being studious and thus well-educated. After finishing that phase of my youth, I was well honed to be a fanatic and eager to prove my zealous ways—to teach what later would be known as *Paulinism*, a universal religion that many would come to know and embrace. But first I had to experience my own conversion, for I was convinced that the new followers of Jesus were a threat to Rome . . .

*For I will shew him how great things he must suffer for my name's sake (Acts 9:16). 10-10-09*

*"Five times I have received at the hands of the Jews the forty lashes less one. Three times I have been beaten with rods; once I was stoned. Three times I have been shipwrecked; a night and a day I have been adrift at sea; on frequent journeys, in danger from rivers, danger from robbers, danger from my own people, danger from Gentiles, danger in the city, danger in the wilderness, danger at sea, danger from false brethren; in toil and hardship, through many a sleepless night, in hunger and thirst, often without food in cold exposure." (2 Cor. 11:24-27).*

*The **Master Hilarion**, Chohan of the 5th Ray incarnate was the **father** of Paul/Saul according to Sharon K. Richards. **Nick Bunick** incarnate was/**is Paul**. See his book: *The Messengers* (1996 & 2006), ISBN# 13: 978-1466477483; 10: 1466477482 for an incredible read.

# TABLE OF CONTENTS

# A SHAKY BEGINNING

I AM Paulus. *Good morning.* So you wish to write a book in conjunction with me. It is a hard task if you decide to do this. *Yes, because I do not know the Bible that well.* So I guess you will learn it, won't you? *Uh-huh.* We have been working together in bringing these words into formation for a book. We will see how it goes. I will direct it, for I still remember that life. I have written two pages (*Prologue*) in which I refute much of what I had done. That will lead the Reader into this controversial book.

Now let us start. *That's the problem, for I do not know the names. With an exasperated sigh, I stopped channeling in order to bring myself more into alignment with this new project I have taken upon myself. 10-26-09*

*Tuesday, October 27, 2009, 7:00 AM. I went into channeling mode after aligning myself with the Father and my gang (the other Masters that guide and teach me). I had no idea of how the session would go. Without Yeshua, I felt I was in a boat without a rudder. I had relied so long on Him that writing a book without His stabilizing influence was a nervous proposition for me. I took a few deep breaths, raised my vibrations the best I could and waited to see what would come across.*

Good morning dear soul, **I AM Paulus**. We will be launching this book this day. I have known for eons of time that there would come a time when I would need to make restitution for the words that I preached throughout the years. There were times when I did not believe what was said, but I believed the Man. Now that may sound strange to you Readers, but remember I was making this leap of faith after being inspired by a Man who was known as a rabble rouser. I was in some ways his defender. In some ways I felt like I was on a crusade. I am sure you have read about people who jump on a bandwagon and take off in their fervor, in their passion. That was the person that I had become.

Much has been written about how I stood and watched while Saint Stephen was martyred and stoned to death. Some of that is true, and I will not deny the fact that I was there. However, the story has been embellished. Remember, even in this day and age there are reporters who report what they see as happening and many times embellish the truth to make a more interesting story—they exaggerate it. This was the case with Saint Stephen. I did not know the man. I was just there. But I did not defend him either, and that is where I grieve. This day and age people come upon youths who are beating someone and they also stand and watch without going to that person's aid. That is what I did; I stood and watched, not knowing particularly why he was being beaten. I only knew he was a follower, a believer in this new religion of Christianity of which I knew little. (*Nick Bunick says he was not present.*)

It is somewhat ironic, for this Stephen became a role model, a template for me—a template that said, *All right, if you are going to carry the Word that is going to be offensive to people, you are going to get into much trouble. You will be stoned, you will be imprisoned, and you could even die.* As you know, that is what happened. But I am telling you the end of the story before I tell you the beginning. (*Actually, he died peacefully in his bed, Nick writes.*)

Let us go back to earlier times. I had extended myself to the authorities and said, *Let me go find these followers who are preaching against the Law. Let me go find them, and I will bring them back so that they can be punished in the Roman way.* And* so, I and some others traveled that road to Damascus. During that time, I had a vision. (*Nick writes it was a business trip only.*)

As a youth, I would have times when I would see things. We now call them *visions*. I did not know what to call them. I would find myself in another place in another time watching, as through a huge glass window, watching a scene unfurl. It would only last a short time, and then I would be back into the present reality. My parents did not know what to make of me. They just thought it must be the fantasy of a child. I soon learned not to talk about the visions. If I did not see a scene, it could be just a face or an object. Many of you do not know that in a meditative state you may see just an object, a ring perhaps. What does it mean? I had no idea.

There were times when I would have these odd dreams, as I came to call them, and I soon learned not to mention them to my parents. It was expected of us if we were in a study period that we would be absorbed in our lessons. Many times that is when the visions would come. As you can see, I was used to having visions.

I was on the road to Damascus. I was on horseback. My horse shied, and I was thrown. All I could see was a brilliant white light. I heard a voice telling me I was no longer to persecute the followers of Jesus. I was to be one of them. I was to give out the Word. I did not even know what the Word was! I did not even know what the message being given to me was about. I only knew I saw this blinding white light. I heard a voice, the strongest I had ever heard, giving me messages, telling me where to go, who to see. This is what my life was going to be about. Some call it being chosen by God. That sounds too ostentatious to me. I put it into the category of, *you brought this with you when you were born; now get on with it! (Nick writes that he did not persecute the followers.)*

It fit right in with my personality—fervor for throwing myself into life's purpose. This book I am writing is not to be a replica of the Bible. It is to help you to understand how a regular person who was raised in a privileged family was molded. How his personality developed. He is what he is. It is religion that claims I was chosen. In actuality, anyone could have stepped up to the plate, as the saying goes. I was never at a loss for words. They came easily to me. I could describe what I saw accurately. There is that saying in your world: *he tells it like it is.*

I learned the Words. I went to the Disciples. You know the story. I went to Peter who saw me for the person that I was, a zealous *born-again*. He did not trust me. And I did not know him. I started listening to what was being taught, and I said the words until they rolled off my tongue. I did not always believe them. I did not always understand them, and I did not always *walk the talk*, as you would say.

I am dead now, as you would put it, although I am an aspect of another soul (*Nick Bunick*). I have integrated into my soul group, and I am aghast at the way *Christianity* and *Paulinism* have taken off down the forked road. One road led the pure way that the Christ spoke of. The other road led to death and destruction, back to the Crusades, the pillaging of the villages, the rapes, stealing the money—all in the name of the Christ. What hypocrisy!

The different sects grew out of Christianity, each one thinking its philosophy was the only way. What hypocrisy. As I look down at your world, if you want to put it into those terms, there is a Saint Paul cathedral, or a Saint Paul chapel, or a Saint Paul city throughout the world. Why—because I brought His word to the Gentiles?

As I look back at my work, it brings tears to this channel's eyes. I see where I was responsible for the distortions of this beautiful way of life. In your day, the Baptists are calling a famous football player names, pointing righteous fingers at him for he had a baby out of wedlock. They are convinced he is going to go to hell. That type of narrow-minded thinking is what keeps Christianity in the lower dimensions, the density of the third dimension. That is third dimension thinking.

How can all of this be made right again—only when people recognize the truth, that there is no sin. There are only bad choices, shall we say. Life is nothing but choices, and the choice you make will be the one that will influence you for the rest of your life.

The devil and Hell are your own creations. There are only choices whether you go to the Light or to the dark; it is a choice.

When you die, you are shown all of your choices and which one could have been the better one or wiser one. You choose even your death. Now if at the time of your death you believe you are going to Hell, that is what you create and that is where you will go in your own fantasy play. You will have a re-play button, and you can replay it over and over. The world is full of thought forms—thoughts that people have of life.

I did not realize it at the time but that is what I was creating, you see, thought forms of what I thought Jesus was saying. People built their own thoughts, so we created this new religion that you will someday remold, rename. Religions need to be updated. That will be a long time in coming.

We will end this chapter for now. There will be much editing required.

I AM Saul of Tarsus.

(*And devout men carried Stephen to his burial and made great lamentation over him. Acts 8:2.*

*As for Saul, he made havoc of the church, entering into every house and hauling men and women committed them to prison. Acts 8:3*)

(*\*Keep in mind that there is much distortion in the Bible. These quotes throughout this book are for reference only, and are not necessarily spoken truth, **or** my beliefs.*)

# CHAPTER 1

# REFLECTION

Good morning, once again I AM Paul. I have just been re-listening to the tape of our session of yesterday. You are still somewhat puzzled as to how this is all going to be enough played out for a book. I no longer can assure you that what I have to say is important or not. It will be up to the Reader. Each Reader will have his or her own way of looking at the world, at religion, and at Saint Paul. Some embrace him while others do not. This channel has a friend, a Jewish friend, who does not like Saint Paul at all. Each of you has your own way of looking at the world and at religion.

After the stoning of Saint Stephen, I withdrew somewhat and went inward. It made me deeply aware that he was a person fervently speaking about a new way of thinking—a new man. You could just feel his heart, for his heart was so involved. So I thought of that, not realizing that at some time on my path, I would be doing the same. I would be preaching out in the market place versus in the synagogues. I would be preaching everywhere I could bring in an audience. I was gifted in that I never seemed to run out of words. I was articulate, and my mind was continuously giving forth information for me to talk about.

As I look back on that now, in my maturity shall we say, in the fact that I have been dead for centuries, I can look back with a more open mind and open heart. Your Lord Jesus the Christ/Yeshua still brings an aura of peace, Light, and forgiveness, which I sorely needed. We now converse and compare notes. He is helping me to see what I could have done differently, where I went off track, for I stepped off the path now and then. But I enjoyed the notoriety and the power. Doors were opened to me then. I was a celebrity, to put it into your words, and I enjoyed it thoroughly.

The danger, you see, is that when you switch from giving a talk of love and you switch to energy of power, then you have changed the energy. You then start drawing to you other people of power. I did not understand the true meaning of love. I talked about it. Many of my words are repeated to this day by people who think that I had spoken them from love. As I look back, the connection was not there. My mind was not connected to the heart and in that way the words were beautiful, so I have been told, but they did not have the substance of love, only authority.

You have that saying that beauty is only skin deep. Words can be the same way. You can speak the word, but the energy behind the word must match. Mine did not always match. I can make excuses for myself and say that I did the best I could with the knowledge that I had, but I must be honest and tell you that I was also greatly influenced by my up-bringing and its strictness of the Pharisaical Laws. My family loved in its own way.

We had divisions and hierarchies in our family. Father was the Patriarch; mother was the Matriarch, and many times it was she who ruled the roost. But we sons did what our father told us to do. We followed in his footsteps, which were not always kind. He loved us in his own way, but he was strict and there was very little praising allowed. We were expected to bow down to the authority in our home. Therefore, when I matured and was out on my own and started to feel this power, I expected people to react to me. I was a leader. I felt like a king walking, telling people how to think, how to do and how to be. The majority of the people were not educated. Therefore, it was I who was teaching them how to be. It was exhilarating!

I parroted the phraseology of Jesus and the Disciples. I had a fine mind and made a brilliant parrot. In retrospect, I loved in my own way. I did not love humanity. I was trying to control and dictate it. Again, people were used to being subjugated, for they did not have the depth of understanding within themselves. They were drawn to Jesus for His love and for His understanding and that realness of Him—what you see is what you get. You saw the love in Jesus, and that is what you got; that is what was returned—unconditional love.

However, when you saw me and heard my words, you did not feel the love. You felt the fervor and the passion: *this is good stuff; you need to learn this!* They were merely being programmed to a different way of thinking. I did not realize at the time that this was a task that I had taken on to bring Yeshua's Words to humanity. I am still not fully recognizing the Words that I spoke.

You see, when someone has a mind such as mine, one learns from watching the repercussions that then happen in one's wake. In a way, I may have brought the Word accurately to the Gentiles, but what they did with it is a sacrilege in itself. How can those scholars, popes, and priests of antiquity preach His Words and my words and still have such evil hearts and evil ways—walking that talk (*molesting the children under their care)?* In the Spanish Inquisitions, if you did not worship God the way they said, you were excommunicated and condemned to death.

Humanity has put me on a pedestal along with Christ. And I say I was merely a follower, one who repeated His Words—a scribe—but I was never on an equal footing. Humanity has put me there. I do not deserve that position. Yes, I loved the Word, loved Him at the time. However, I am not a martyr as the Bible would have you believe, for as I was saying, I am not His equal. Please do not think I just am being modest. I am being truthful. I have had centuries to think about it.

The purpose of this book is to provide you Readers with a different perspective. Read His Words and glorify those! Do not make me a saint for repeating them with my passion. I must come from love and truth and match the heart. I did the best I could with the tools that I had, shall we say. I wish I could have done better. And I ask for His forgiveness for the errors of my ways.

I AM Paulus.

*(For I speak to you Gentiles, inasmuch as I am the apostle of the Gentiles, I magnify mine office. Ro 11:13.)*

# CHAPTER 2

# PAULUS MUSES

**I AM Paulus.** *The book is coming along nicely, and I am most pleased. We will be getting down into the knitty gritty of it shortly. I have set this book up so that I will talk about my life and my struggles, and then I will bring forth other actors of that play and let them speak or forever hold their peace. Now I must admit I am at a loss for words, for in the first few pages I was telling you everything that I was not! I was not the man who carried the Word from love of his heart. I was a messenger but still a neophyte. I molded the Words that I heard to my own way. I molded it to what I thought Yeshua would say.*

How does one approach transmuting various segments of one's past life? For me, I have been thinking about it for a long time. I go back in my mind to the different times in my life. Where did I not hear correctly? Where could I have made it truer?

Each one of you Readers has had past lives, whether you believe it or not. It is true, for you have come from different star systems as we all have. We then settled on Planet Earth in order to take up a new assignment from the Father to help bring this planet into consciousness.

Back in those ancient days of antiquity, Yeshua was the one who carried the Light for the planet, shall we say. Others may have been points of Light from different indigenous peoples throughout the world, but my little world was just that, a little world that encompassed the lands that you now call Israel and much of the Greek Islands that I visited. I walked thousands of miles. History has said that I covered 8000 miles, either walking, running, (*horses*) or by ship—always with a zest for life, getting into dangerous situations, being beaten, thrown into chains, into solitary confinement. It was similar to a movie. If you were making a movie and threw in all the negative situations, it was as though I were experiencing each segment of that.

I had no real fear. (It sounds as if I was either fearless or clueless or both!) I found myself in one bad situation after another. And of course I could not hold my tongue. Therefore, it would lead me hither and yon, positive and negative. Such judgmental arrogance, for I always knew best (*smile*). Bit by bit the Word—those beautiful Words of Yeshua—spread throughout the area, our world.

Now let us go to the Bible and see what we can do here. This channel does not know the Bible that well, but I will guide her to different passages. I wish for her to pick up her Bible at this point and to turn to Acts 13.

(*Chako: It was at this point that I felt myself rising into confusion. I read Acts 13 and did not know what to do with it. I was not sure I was hearing what Paul said. I had been sitting for an hour so I decided, "OK, this is enough for today; I'll see if I can pick it up tomorrow." So hang in there with me, Readers. I have no idea what's coming next! 11-07-09, 10:45 AM.*)

*Sunday, November 8, 2009, 8:50 AM.* Good morning precious one. Shall we try again? *Yes, (laughingly) we shall try!* I see you have the Bible open to Acts 13. *Yes.* Now let us try it a little differently. You have read the chapter. *Yes.* Scroll down to where Paul is teaching.

*Acts 13:47 For so hath the Lord commanded us saying, I have set thee to be a Light of the Gentiles that thou shouldest be for salvation unto the ends of the Earth.*

*Acts 13:50 But the Jews stirred up the devout and honorable women and the chief men of the city, and raised persecution against Paul and Barnabas and expelled them out of their coasts.*

Therefore, Barnabas and I were not received well by the Jews. It would have been dangerous had we stayed, so we left. That was only one of many confrontations that we had as we attempted to continue with our task. I often asked why I continued. Why did I not just stop preaching this Word that I knew little about? But I had this drive. I do not know if this was my purpose. I did not know about things like that. I just had this drive that propelled me forward.

During the course of my journeys I met many people. As I traveled further away from Jerusalem, fewer and fewer people had heard of Jesus, so I was not only teaching them about the Word, but about the Man of which I knew little. However, the Apostles had talked about Him so much that I felt I knew Him somewhat also. I do not know where this great passion for Him came from—unless it was the fact that I spoke so often of Him that I actually had called forth His energy. Consequently, I felt wrapped in His embrace. (*Nick Bunick writes that he had met and conversed frequently with Yeshua.*)

There were healings that I did. I did them only because I could—not because I felt particularly sorry for that person. There were so many who were disabled and ignorant that I just picked and chose. I cannot say that I healed them, per se, for actually their own energy was called forth. They just needed guidance.

One day I saw this man. He literally had a white film over his eyes. I knew he was blind and not a fraud. So I chose him to heal, not knowing if the words would work or not. It was in that category of *oh what the heck; let's give it a try.* I think I was as astounded as he when his eyes cleared—weakly at first and then gradually his sight became stronger and stronger. I was quite surprised, but truly very glad for him. *It was kind of neat,* I thought. My excitement was for the fact that I in some way was able to do this, not because

I particularly loved the man. The difference was that Jesus/Yeshua loved first, and then He activated the healing.

I have come to the end of my story telling, and it is now time for others to step forth and to give their version of this play. I AM Paulus

*Go thy way (Ananias), for he is a chosen vessel unto me, to bear my name before the Gentiles, and kings, and the children of Israel (Acts 9:15).*

# CHAPTER 3

# YESHUA SPEAKS

*Good morning, my precious one; you had a bit of trouble getting back into the swing of things, but not giving up. All is not down the tubes. It will fall into place. Keep your hopes up, dear one; it will fall into place.*

*Now you were wondering about this Entity that you were channeling. The Entity* **is** *Saint Paul. So just relax and know what he has said to you is truth. Let him speak some more when he wishes to. You were trying to put a square peg into a round hole again, and it did not fit so you got a little off track. Relax and let it flow again. You last left it where that was the end of your story for now and to let others come forth. Why don't we do that—let another speak. (Thank you; get me out of this log-jam.)*

All right, dear one, **I AM Yeshua,** as you have figured out by now. I have come to give you a chapter for your book that perhaps will help you to go forward. We will name this chapter *Yeshua Speaks.*

Throughout the eons of time since that Biblical era, Saint Paul, or Paulus, and I have met many times talking over what went on, what could have gone on, what went wrong, and how could it have been made better. Basically we were airing where we came from from both sides of the coin.

Paulus realizes now after the fact, which so often happens when one dies, that he had gotten off track. He realizes that he had gone into ego and power and that he did not always have his followers' best interests at heart. But basically, Readers, he was what you would call a *good man*. He was developing his heart such as many of you are. It has been said many times that people love at different levels. Those who truly love deeply have a fully developed heart of love, while others have what we call a *shallow heart*. They can only love just so deep. Many times when a person is so full of passion and fervor for his/her cause, he goes forth and does not realize that he is coming from a shallow heart, for he is more into his head, you see. He is more into his ego, which is actually serving him. His mind becomes the master and not the heart—such as it was with Paulus. His mind was the master.

I know this may shock many of you people, especially if you are deeply into religion, for you can barely say a Biblical verse without quoting Paul. He had great articulation; he was an orator. He knew how to express himself. What were lacking were love, the gentleness, and the caring. He did not have that. I will say he did not carry that.

However, I cannot condemn him for that. He was a human being. He was on assignment and was doing the best that **he** knew how. Unfortunately, since it did not come from the heart, his messages became distorted. As he has said to you, there was a fork in the road, and he went down one way and my teachings that I gave were down another road.

Yes, he was the bridge between the Jews and the Gentiles. He did bring my Words forth. But when they become platitudes, when they do not carry the depth of love, then that is all they are—just words. There was enough Light in there that the energy went forth so that my Words did go throughout the world, however.

I became angry when I saw how my teachings had become distorted. However, I must draw back because, although he was very passionate and verbal, he actually in that sense taught what

I had said a little differently than the other Disciples, the other Apostles. He is known as the 13th Apostle—Paulus.

Know if you had 13 friends and you sat in a circle and you said to them give me a paragraph on my teachings, you would find that each Apostle would have a different perspective. Some of the Apostles did not have an education. Therefore, their perspective would come from the wisdom, we would say, of a fisherman. And he was correct in the way he interpreted my words because they were meant for that particular strata of people. It would be similar to going to a lecture by a great scientist and then coming away trying to figure out what in the world did he say, because you were not a physicist.

Therefore, when Paulus spoke, you could say that he spoke as the 13th Apostle and reached a different stratum of people. He was highly educated. This is one of the reasons why he was not able to teach the Rabbis, the Jewish educators, because he said the teachings in a way that they could not understand. Many of those Rabbis were highly educated, as was Paulus, but here is an educated man taking the Words from **me.** I was speaking to the common man in my common language—Aramaic. He took that common way of speaking to a higher level so that people could not understand him. To this day there are passages that Paulus has said that people do not understand—again his brilliant mind.

Consequently, I was angry for I saw him raise the level of my teachings to a more advanced way of perceiving. In that sense, you see, it was way over the heads of the common man, and over the heads of the Jews. Many times in the passages in Paulus' epistles you will see how he speaks repeatedly on one theme, especially on *circumcision. (Ro. 2:25,26,27,28,29; 3:1,30; 4:9,10,11,12; 15:8; 1Co 7:19; Col 2:11; 3:11; 4:11)* He spoke repeatedly on it, tried it from all angles, trying to get people to realize that if a Gentile was following the Laws in his own way—the moral Laws, we'll say—and he was not circumcised, was he not still at the level of a circumcised Jew? Why did it matter? People to this day do not understand his reasoning on that one.

So here was Paulus speaking with ego-passion from the mind. Another point of his teachings was that he put me on such a high godlike level that I was no longer considered part of mankind. I wanted to be the hu-man. I wanted to be the next-door neighbor. I wanted to be the fisherman in the market place. I wanted to be the worshipper at the feet of another teacher. I wanted to be just a man, but coming from the Father's principles—coming from love, coming from forgiveness.

Many of the people were into revenge. You did something to them and boy, would you get it back again. They never understood my teaching of turning the other cheek, blessing the person who had harmed you and asking God the Father to take over. It was not up to you. People did not understand that. Now here comes Paulus, and he is just raring to go. He was ignorant of my strategy as to where I was coming from. All he knew were the Words that I had said, and he did not have the depth of understanding to know what I was referring to, what I had in mind—what I was trying to elicit from my followers.

You know, when we put ourselves out there as a teacher, we have in mind that what we say will elicit a response from the person or the people we are talking to. The response that we are hoping for them is that the teachings would bring them to a new level of consciousness, that they would have that light bulb turn on, that *ah-ha* effect. That is what we as teachers are always hoping will happen with the students, or the followers, or the audience. Therefore, to have someone such as Paul not grasp the meaning either—in that way the message became distorted, making me a God, versus a Man.

Of course you know by now, readers of this book, that we are all gods in our own right because we are all one. We are part of the God-Father. We are all one! But you see, the populace at that time did not know that. Therefore, they had to make that separation. Instead of bringing people in as One as I was attempting to do, Paul made the separation even more so by raising me up above everyone else. Then people might get the meaning more easily. Not!

I am a brother to you. I am one with you. Yes, I may have skills that you do not have. I may have knowledge that you do not have, but I am still one of you. I am a brother in your family. We are a family! Many people after they read this book will be choosing sides, shall we say. When I told you that I was angry with Paul for getting off track, then **they** will be angry with him. That is not the object of this chapter. It is to point out the discrepancies. It is to have you discern.

Even so, Paulus, yes, was a great man. He had passion for what he did. Yes, he brought my Word out to the world. But people, bring that into perspective, for you have not only made him a saint, but you have also made **him** a god. That is not correct thinking either. He was a man with passion. He saw something that sparked the great knowledge within him, and he went after it. Do not condemn him for his judgment, for his way of addressing, going forth with a purpose, and remaining steadfast.

He was a man with a mission, one who went throughout the world. He is on every Biblical scholar's lips alongside my name. He is my brother as much as all of you are my brothers and sisters. Do we always like our brothers and sisters, even in our intimate families? NO. We argue; we fight; we disagree, but basically if anyone should do harm to our sibling, we would be the first to jump in to protect him/her.

Your Paulus has become my friend. I love him as a brother. He has asked for my forgiveness. Of course I have given it to him. Why would I not? He was a hu-man being such as I was in those days of antiquity. All I can say, Readers, if you think living in today's world is difficult, you ought to have tried it back then—and many of you did. Goodness sake! 2000+ years ago!

So, our dear Readers, I came this morning to continue Paulus' story. It is true. Everything he has said to you is true. Do not be dismayed. Open your hearts and realize that he was not different from any of you. It is a past life we are talking about. How many of you have had past lives? It was a past life. He has earned merit; he has earned gold stars. He did well and he did not so well, but he learned, and he was willing to give his life for his belief—was willing to give his life in order to bring my Word to all of you. That was a beautiful gift in itself. I receive it with honor and great love. Not everyone who gives us gifts gives as unselfishly as Paulus has done. He said he felt he had not earned the Sainthood that the Pope has bestowed on him. I say he did the very best that he knew how; he gave his very best and that is all that we can ever ask of anyone given an assignment—to give your best in joy and love.

I AM Yeshua.

*(Thank you Lord; it was truly wonderful.)* You are welcome, dear one; you are welcome.

*(For circumcision verily profiteth, if thou keep the law: but if thou be a breaker of the law thy circumcision is made uncircumcision Ro2:25.*

*Therefore, if the uncircumcision keeps the righteousness of the law, shall not his uncircumcision be counted for circumcision? Ro 2:26)*

# CHAPTER 4

# PAUL'S DEATH

Good morning, our precious one; we have come once again to continue this book. **I AM Saint Paul**; some say *Saul of Tarsus*; some say *Paulus*, my Roman name, or *Paul*. I was delighted to have Yeshua come and speak as beautifully as he did on my life, on my abilities and my disabilities. We have had many conversations about that lifetime.

(*I know, Readers, you must be wondering what the truth about Paul's death was. The Bible leads one to believe that he was in prison when he died. Another school of thought claims he was beheaded. According to Nick Bunick, he was under house arrest. The house had a back garden and Paul spent much time there, writing, receiving visiting friends and eventually died peacefully in his own bed. Read* The Messengers {2006} *for more information.*)

No one particularly enjoys the critique of his/her life that is now a past life, because all that you did not accomplish and all that you did not do correctly according to your contract (*took some side trips off the path, perhaps*) is now critiqued by you and your higher souls. You are the judge of you, continues Paul.

I then saw the error of my ways. One does not expect accolades for a lifetime. It was a huge assignment, a huge undertaking, and I saw that some of what I had done was positive in nature and other parts of it were not so positive. Of course hindsight is always more advantageous, but it was painful to sit and watch my every move, my thoughts, my emotions and the body's reactions. I watched it all as in a play and felt every scene.

Seldom is a life's review done in just a few minutes or one day. You sit and the hours go by rapidly, and you are not aware of how long you have spent. It could have been several days or weeks and perhaps several months. While this is going on, one is being instructed and being taught and reconnecting with the higher parts of oneself. I did not experience Purgatory or Hell, for my thoughts were so full of the Lord Jesus Christ I just knew I would be seeing Him. That is just what happened. I saw this Light and felt His love. I went to Him and fell upon my knees. He said very little. I did not hear what so many Christians are praying fervently for, "Well done, my good and faithful servant." I did not hear that. I merely heard, "Thank you, Paul, for your service to Me."

I remember then being led to the healing chamber, laying down and going to sleep. Here it is the year of 2012. Death is no longer permitted in the more **civilized** countries of the world for speaking one's religious beliefs, although a few countries still maintain a strict code of what one can speak if it is considered blasphemous. There is religious freedom in America of sorts. However, there can be much judgment and intolerance still. Although humanity has moved forward in technology, many people are very slow in their emotional maturity, in their spiritual beliefs—which will lead them back to the Father.

During that Biblical lifetime, I had a great friend in Barnabas. We traveled extensively carrying the Word of the Lord Jesus Christ. We did not always get along and had our differences, which led eventually to parting company. However, I still recognize him as a friend. Therefore, we will ask Barnabas to come forward for the next chapter. I AM Paul (4-64 C.E.)

*O death where is thy sting? O grave where is thy victory? (1 Co 15:55)*

(Author: This is as good a place as any to give you more information. About 15 years ago I had a dream where I was writing in my *Book of Life*. I wrote *Kent-Kent, Saint Paul*. I had wondered for years what my connection to Paul was, or even if I may be an aspect of him. It was not until I had had a reading with Sharon K. Richards that Yeshua told me I was a leader of one of Paul's churches. This is significant in that I was a woman, Mariam, Yeshua's adopted cousin-sister and had taught his Words to many. The men were slower to receive this teaching from a woman who knew more than they did, having studied with the Essenes, and having achieved initiations while in Egypt with Mary Magdalene and Yeshua.)

Read more about Mariam in *Anna, Grandmother of Jesus* by Claire Heartsong and *Anna: The Voice of the Magdalenes* by Claire Heartsong and Catherine Ann Clemett. Amazon.com carries these books.

I have left the following page blank for any notations you might care to make.

# NOTATIONS

# CHAPTER 5

# BARNABAS

Good morning, dear Readers, **I AM Barnabas**, a companion of Saul of Tarsus (*a city larger than Athens, Greece and what is now present day Turkey*). We became great friends and shared a passion for spreading Jesus' Words. Now the Bible does not always report accurately what was said, but it is close enough. Paul and I were friends. We had our differences. He thought we ought to go there and I thought we ought to go here. I seemed to always acquiesce to him. I would always go where Paul went.

We were not always treated kindly. People stared at us, laughed at us, made crude remarks. I did not understand the teachings. If Jesus were there, He would have been teaching in parables. I did not do that. Paul did most of the talking. You can read his epistles. He does not speak in parables either.

Paul was not married. There was no room for a wife in his life. He did not want to have to share his time with another like he would have to do if he were a husband. Therefore, he really did not learn a woman's point of view. He did not learn the enjoyment of having conversations with a woman. We would be speaking of the Goddess energy, would we not? He was not allowing that for he was coming from the masculine principle.

You know when you think you are always right (*laughing*), it is very difficult to get another idea into your head. That is the way it was with Paul. He molded what he thought about women from his family upbringing. His father was the Patriarch. Consequently, Paul thought that women always ought to subjugate themselves to the men. I guess you would say that Paul was not a *women's libber.* If one were to ask if Paul respected women, it would be in the category that they are necessary for the bearing of children, to propagate the family, but for having one as a companion such as Mary Magdalene was to Yeshua, that was not in his reality. Some people think he was a homosexual. He was not, although as you know from these books, each person will have a homosexual life in order to learn the masculine and Goddess principles. However, that was not Paul's purpose that lifetime.

He prayed a great deal. I think he must have been in emotional agony at times, for you cannot have such passion and fervor without having your body wanting physical touch. Many men in that era enjoyed the services of the prostitutes, but Paul did not. Whether he had before his conversion, I do not know. He focused himself on his mission, and as I've said, prayed a lot (smile).

Anyone who was a prophet or a teacher in those times of antiquity took a life that was most difficult. Many times they did not honor their body, per se. They did not give it that much attention. Look at John the Baptist, eating bugs and wearing animal clothing. He was far into the spiritual realm but also mostly out of his body.

Thus Paul abused his body in that he was not conscious of it—his diet was very poor. His body was very strong, although he ignored it the best he could and prayed to God for strength to keep on ignoring it. He was growing his heart. He never achieved a full, loving heart because he would not let the Goddess energy in. You men out there, you need your feminine side, your Goddess side, if you are going to have a full, deep heart. You women out there, you need your masculine side, your masculine energy, in order to be balanced also. Life is a balance, is it not? We can get so caught up with our mission, our passion that we forget that we are to be in balance.

Paul and I are still friends. Our connection is of that one lifetime. At first we were a team. We were both learning; we were neophytes at being the traveling preachers, so to speak. Then Paul's passion overtook his reason. He slid more into power and control. We were no longer a team, and that is when we decided to end our partnership. It was a wrenching split, for we were both angry. He went his way and I went mine. This is all I wish to say for now.

Thank you for this opportunity to speak with you Readers. I AM Barnabas.

*And the contention was so sharp between them that they departed asunder one from the other . . . (Acts 15:39)*

*(Author: Jose or Joseph Barnabas, a Levite of Cyprus, was sent by the Apostles to Antioch to confirm the church there. From there he went to Tarsus to seek Saul, for he had introduced him to Peter, James, and John in Jerusalem as a new convert. Barnabas traveled with Paul on his first missionary journey.)*

# CHAPTER 6

# PETER CRITIQUES PAUL

*All right, dearest one; I AM Yeshua. You were discussing with Paul yesterday whether this book you are writing together was finished or not. First, I would like to congratulate you for the excellent job you and Paul have been doing. The book is beautifully constructed and very informative and, shall I say, "right on!" The truth that you are willing to speak about is commendable.*

*I feel that there could be a few more Presenters, so instead of putting out a pamphlet, you really will have a little book, and I am willing to do this for you since you have asked.* (Oh thank you Lord, yes, yes, yes!!) *Therefore, let us bring in some other players in that drama.*

*Paul was taken to Jerusalem and presented to the Council there, consisting of the Apostles Peter, John, and James. Peter was not too welcoming, for he had heard about the mud slinging that Paul before his conversion had done to the people who embraced My Words. So let us bring Peter forth and hear his story, and then I will come back.* (Oh gosh, thank you, Yeshua.) *You are welcome, dear one.*

Hello dear soul, **I AM Peter.** (*Hello, Lord.*) You wish to have me say a few words about my discussion with Paul, what I thought of him and what came out of our meeting? (*Yes, please.*) Well my first impression when I saw him was that he was a man with a mission.

He had such zeal that it was rather astounding, for I had been so used to talking with people who were less enthusiastic about hearing my words. They were not particularly laid back; they could just care less. Then here comes a man to me who is just burning as with a fever, wanting to know as much as he possibly could about our Lord's work. He was not overly tall. His dark eyebrows joined together as if always in a continuous concentration. He moved quickly; he thought quickly, and he spoke quickly.

I would start a sentence and he would almost finish it for me, for he grasped so eagerly what I was conveying. He wanted to know everything about Yeshua. He asked numerous questions. He wanted to know what his habits were; he wanted to know if he laughed a lot. He wanted to know what he ate and if he had any food addictions, as if that made a difference. But you see, back in that era there were many people who were addicted to the fruits of the vine.

He wanted to know how people received him, how they perceived him. He wanted to know about his family; who were his brothers and sisters—where were they and what were they doing now. Then after he absorbed all of that, he wanted to know about the various teachings—all that I could possibly remember. When he was more or less satiated with that, he returned and asked more questions about the teachings. He met James and John also and asked them similar questions.

We met for several days at a time and Paul was always questioning, always wanting to know more. It was as if we would tell him one thing and that would lead off to something else. It amazed me, for he was not what I was expecting. He was a scholar and he was not dull in any respect. He had a mind like a trap. You put something in it and it trapped shut. The danger in that, however, is that when he had made up his mind about certain subjects, there was little room for flexibility. There was little room to maneuver or to change his perspective in any way.

He drew in some way his own ideas about what we were saying. He did not think of himself at that time as the 13th Apostle. That label was put on him years later. He felt more as an outsider, and we looked upon him as an outsider. We had this tight-knit group. The Holy Spirit had come upon all of us. Paul was still a neophyte. He was someone who wanted to pick our brains, so to speak, and then go forth and shout it to the world in **his** way. It disturbed us. While he had the teachings and the concepts in his bear-trap mind, his heart seemed to be lacking. His zealousness was so prevalent.

I make a reference, dear Readers, to many of you. Look back at yourself when you were first turning on and getting excited about all the New Age and psychic realms. You were so excited when you were able to do this and then able to do that. You heard about this teaching and you heard about that teaching. You were an avid reader and you would clean the psychic books off the library shelves. You attended any group that was presenting subjects along the psychic lines. You were struck with the most powerful drive to obtain as much information as you possibly could. Now put yourself back into Paul's shoes. He was no different. It was not the psychic drive that was feeding him; it was learning the Word, knowing the Christ. That is what he wanted, and he could not get enough knowledge of Him. He was burning for it. You take his superfine mind, one that could create thoughts and articulate, and he could intimidate others easily.

Many of the Apostles had a hard time with him for there was no way that they could match his knowledge. He had traveled a great deal. Goodness sakes, he had traveled extensively! Some of the Apostles had not been out of their own little area. Paul could espouse on almost any subject. The Apostles would ask him questions "well what about this; what did you see when you did that, etc." He gave very quick replies and then he would come right back at them with his own agenda, wanting more, pulling, pulling more information from them.

We did not quite know what to make of him. I must say the judgments that we went into were not all that positive. We'd say, *"My gosh, this man is going to go forth and he is going to carry the*

*Word. He has all these ideas about the Gentiles not having to be circumcised and here we were trying to teach the Word to the Jews.”* We were all circumcised, and it was as though he was in a different world than ours. In some respects he was and it was scary to us.

Therefore, we made an agreement. “OK, Paul, you go out and you teach the Gentiles Jesus’ Words. If they do not want to be circumcised but will love Him and His Words, then OK. But we will continue to teach the Jews. We will continue to follow the Law of Moses.” That is what we did. We taught it in the *circumcised* way and let Paul go off in his way. (Bear in mind, Paul was a circumcised Jew.)

History claims that I, Peter, was the first to spread the Word, but you see, my area was not as vast as Paul’s, and he literally reached out to the world. We did not have television, newspapers or anything of that sort, of course. All we had was almost like a *runner*—similar to the American Indians who would run from one camp to another carrying a message. That was the way it was with Paul—carrying the message, loving everything about it.

We often would exclaim among ourselves, *my gosh, you cannot kill this man!* Someone would give him a verbal dressing down or beat him down, and he would pop right up again. You can’t keep him down. So we made it to the point that we could live with. “All right we’ll do it our way. You go out into **your** part of the world, and you do it your way as long as you stay true to Yeshua’s Words, and stay true to His teachings.”

As I look back in history, both ways worked, did they not? There are still Evangelists who are Jews, and they are teaching their Jewish parishioners the Word of Jesus. They are compatible; Jesus was a Jew. He kept the Laws and this is what He said. That was more in my comfort zone. I was not comfortable going outside my comfort zone by eating a meal prepared by the Gentiles. I was not able to do that. Whereas Paul, who was a few years younger than Yeshua, was ecstatic when a Gentile asked him to share a meal. “That is a wonderful time to go and talk about the man, Jesus.”

While we had an agreement, it was an agreement with conditions. As long as Paul would stay true to the Word, then he was welcome to spread the Word. As history has proved, he did it brilliantly. Most of the New Testament is from Paul. He did it brilliantly. I only can commend him for that. We were never friends, per se. I guess you could say we were colleagues in our own fashion. We respected each other each in his own way, with limitations (*smile*) and judgments. As I look back at history, he was a man who changed the religious world; he changed history. In that simple life, some say unselfishly given, a life where he gave little to himself—every thought, every word, every deed was with Yeshua in mind.

Yes, Paul stepped off the path as he grew in power. He loved the Lord Jesus Christ as much as he could love anyone, as much as he could love anyone, including himself.

Thank you for this opportunity to give you a little bit more of the picture of the 13th Apostle as I now call him. He deserves your appreciation for all that he has done. Yes, there is much back-pedaling to do, making the wrongs into rights. That is what this book is all about. He tried. At least he tried, Readers.

I AM Peter. (*Thank you, Saint Peter.*)

*All right that was our friend, Peter—on this rock I shall build my church (chuckle)—and now we have to re-establish his church with a new foundation. It will be slow in coming for there is much distortion in the Christian religion, but this book is a start; it is a start. 'til later, dear one, I AM Yeshua. (And when Saul was come to Jerusalem, he assayed to join himself to the disciples, but they were all afraid of him and believed not that he was a disciple. Acts 10:26).*

# CHAPTER 7

# YESHUA'S PERSPECTIVE

Good morning to our Readers, **I AM Yeshua**. As you can see, there has been a little change—a change of plans (*chuckles*) in the way we are preceding with this book. This channel and Paul thought they had more or less come to the end of **their** road, but they still felt that the book was not finished. Consequently, they asked me for help, and of course I gladly am giving it. I will now see them to the end of this book because it will be quite a glorious book, and it is meant to awaken many people.

So many people idolize Saint Paul. In some ways they are not wrong. In some ways he brought the Word, the teachings forth. Of course it was not all his fault that the teachings became distorted. People have free will, and they think what they think. Therefore, they elevated Paul to the level where they had elevated me, to be a God. They have Paul right at my heels.

He was a great man in his own way, Readers. How many of you would have taken my teaching—say if I were teaching a class—how many of you would have taken my teaching and would have run with it throughout different countries? Yes, his interpretation was his, but at least he was trying. At least he was being of service. He did not realize that it was being of service at the time. He just was so thrilled with the Word. He had such passion and drive.

Now some of this was from his pre-birth contract that had finally de-coded for him. He felt that this was his purpose. He felt that this was what he needed to do with the rest of his life. What is so amazing about this, Readers, and I want you to really hear this, is that he was willing to give up his life for the Word—for his trust in me. He was willing to give his body and soul to this work.

He was beaten; I do not know how many times. He was thrown into jail with very little to eat, and you know back in those days the filth and lack of sanitation must have been very painful for someone who had been raised with a silver spoon. How difficult this was for him, and yet he did it; he did it! And then he wrote beautifully of his thoughts.

Yes, I can be angry at times when the Word did not go out as I had envisioned it to be. But he was a human being, and he was trying his best. I cannot condemn him for that. All of us can only do our best with the consciousness that we carry at that time.

Dear Readers, this book has been fairly heavy on the negative aspects of Paul. However, just know he was not all bad; he was not all wrong. He was just somewhat distorted in his beliefs. But keep in mind, the passion never wavered; his passion went on. In fact, it seems as though the more he was tried and ostracized and beaten into submission, he never submitted. He popped back again with fervor, even more so, to carry forward toward his goal.

He did not think in terms that he may be killed. That would have been too much to bear. But he knew he was going to die; he just did not know how. Everyone knows he is going to die, although that is no longer necessary as you have been told, as you go toward making your body immortal in the higher dimensions.

Back in antiquity, Paul was struggling with a third—dimensional body. Some of the people he was with were only in the second dimension. I cannot emphasize enough the lack of consciousness that was in the majority of the people during that time. You see, what I knew and Paul did not know was that these people with the lower consciousness were Divine Beings. They had become so engrossed with physicality that they had forgotten who they were and did not know we were all brothers and sisters, and they did not know I was no higher than they were.

They made me into a God. Those who followed Paul heard his teachings that had been shaped now by his own belief systems. They heard that, and then down through the generations, the Christian movement became like a surge. The Catholic popes possessed the teachings and deified Paul; canonized Paul, all of which he may have deserved for the service he had done.

When you finish this book, leave your heart open and think about him in the generation that **he** lived. Do not think about Paul in the present Now of 2012. He would have been entirely different then—but not so different from that man now. *(Actually, he now is in the body of Nick Bunick who is a successful, wealthy business man, as was Paul. Nick, through many sessions of past-life regression came to accept the fact that indeed he was/is Saint Paul.)*

He was a great man who was overpowered by his zeal in life. He started to enjoy the power and the notoriety. He was a man on a mission. He followed through to his end and had a peaceful death. Now if he had stayed on the path and had stayed true to my Words and understood what I was saying and was navigating in the level that I was teaching, would he have died differently? In those days of antiquity, the great prophets, the great teachers, all were killed—killed by those with the mentality that did not understand. We will never know.

It would be similar, Readers, now in 2012. People are worried about spaceships and that aliens are coming to take them over and to do experiments on them. If one of the ships landed, people would stone it or shoot it down—shoot first and we will find out who you are later. So you see, there is a huge gap here, a huge gap in consciousness still. The technology can be there but the consciousness of so many is still at the third dimension level. You are creating your bodies for the 4th dimension and into the 5th. And you cannot do it unless your thought processes rise up so that you are at a higher consciousness.

The world will not be the same year after year. The world is going through its changes and you must change with it, or you can work from what we call the *other side*, as Paul did. He told you how he had his life's review. Time is different on that side (*Galactic versus linear*). It is just one other thing that souls do. He is a great part of the Biblical crowd, we shall say—*a member of my soul group.*

Let us call this Chapter 7 *Yeshua's Perspective*. Now let us bring in another Presenter, for this book is not finished. Let us bring in Saint Luke for he also was a companion to Paul. We will let him tell his story (*continued in Chapter 8.*)

(*Thank you Yeshua.*) You are welcome, dear one.

(*And when Barnabas had found Saul, he brought him into Antioch. And it came to pass that a whole year they assembled themselves with the church and taught much people. And the disciples were called* Christians *first in Antioch. Acts 11:26).*

(*Love is patient; love is kind. It does not envy; it does not boast; it is not proud. It is not rude; it is not self-seeking; it is not easily angered; it keeps no record of wrongs. Love does not delight in evil but rejoices with the truth. It always protects, always trusts, always hopes, always perseveres 1Corinthians 13:4-7).*

(Author: Theologians to this day agree that Paul's words on true love have rarely been equaled for its truth and simplicity.)

# CHAPTER 8

# SAINT LUKE COMMENTS

Good morning, Readers, and to this channel, I am the soul known as Saint Luke, and I was a friend to Saint Paul. I ministered to him frequently when he was under arrest. I was a physician even then. I brought him powders and teas to drink to help him. He suffered from what you would call *allergies*. There was so much dust and dirt and mold in those places where Paul was imprisoned.

His nose was always running; his sinuses ached and his body was miserable at times. He could not get warm enough. Therefore, he threw himself into his writing, for he said when he wrote, he could forget where he was and forget his body was *betraying him*, as he would put it. He prayed a great deal and that helped, for at those times he could leave his body, and that gave him a few hours of peace.

You Readers that think he just sat and wrote; you do not know of the anguish he was experiencing many times. He may not have had a deep heart, but the heart that he had gave him emotional struggles. Just as all of you have struggled with your emotional bodies, he was no different. In fact, his emotions were intensified by the great passion that he carried.

When I visited him, he liked to hear of the *outside world* as he put it, for he was so confined—two years in one room with little to eat. He was an avid reader and he could lose himself among the books. He was always asking me to bring him books to help fill the time, to help him from becoming mentally ill. So he wrote and he read, and he wrote and he read.

He told me about his life growing up, how strict his parents were. He did not feel their love for him. That is the way most privileged children were raised in those days with strict rules. He knew no different. When you have an upbringing like that, it does not give you much opportunity to grow the depth of your own heart, does it? And yet he did reach out to people; he reached out and people were touched by him.

When he was not in prison, he had the healing aura around him. People were healed. History has it that any handkerchiefs that he carried on his person would be filled with so much of his energy that as he gave them to people they would be healed. He did not speak of that particularly, for his thoughts were mostly on Jesus and His Words.

We would actually have discussions trying to figure out what do you think He meant by this passage? We could never quite figure out that the Kingdom of God was within, for we were making it too physical, you see. We could not grasp what Jesus meant by that.

I was not always with Paul, but the times that I was became meaningful for me. I guess you could say we had a meeting of the minds. People of that caliber were so few and far between that you could debate with and argue with and exchange ideas with. He was so quick. When I told him about some of my medical cases, he was very interested and would ask astute questions.

I grieved when I had heard that the authorities had taken him away. I felt hollowness in my soul. He was a friend and I missed him; I missed him. I prayed for him. He was a good man, worthy of my prayers. I bless him when I think of him.

I AM Luke

*Thank you Saint Luke for your words.* You are welcome. You did the best that you could teaching the Word, as much as you were allowed to. Let history speak for itself.

I am finished.

(*Wherefore, let him that thinketh he standeth take heed lest he fall. 1Co 10:12.*

*There hath no temptation taken you but such as is common to man; but God is faithful, who will not suffer you to be tempted above that ye are able; but will with the temptation also make a way to escape, that ye may be able to bear it. 10:13*).

# CONCLUSION

# YESHUA & PAULUS

Good morning my brothers and sisters, **I AM Yeshua,** coming to you on this glorious day in Arizona. I come this morning to continue this book, which has a purpose, a very great purpose, for it is the start of releasing incorrect information—releasing incorrect dogma from the Christian religious world.

Not many people will be willing to let go of their preconceived ideas. They have heard it for so long, so long that they wish to keep the same ideas going—even keeping the idea of Armageddon, which, my dear Readers, is not true.

Today we will be speaking more about the life of the man who is called *Saint Paul*. I honor him by saying this, for he took many insults that were laid upon him all in My Name. He tried his very best and, while he did not always speak the thoughts that I myself had put forth, he did convey the subject matter to the best of his ability. He was teaching a new language, you see. He was teaching a new language to people—a completely new language.

Put yourself, perhaps, back in Antiquity and say to yourself that you are going to go listen to this man who has been talking about Jesus. You had your own ideas. You are a Gentile. You had your way of living, your own programmed religion, or maybe you didn't even think you had a religion.

And you went to hear this man. It was a totally new language for you, for he used terms that made no sense to you. He talked about a God. Many of you did not believe in a God then. The Jews would not even say his name. They used different terms, such as *All That Is*. They heard this man who they knew as *Paulus*, for he used his Roman name. They heard him say that the *Kingdom of God is within*. To their minds, a Kingdom was an area where a King had a castle. To say that God was a King and that he lived inside of your heart was beyond their understanding. Many people to this day cannot understand this either.

There was something, some energy in the Words that drew people to come and listen to Paul. He was a great orator and he had a way with words. In your present day you have your President Barack Obama who is also an orator. He too gets faulted if he speaks above the heads of people. They call him an *elitist* then and not one for the common man.

Paul knew no different. If you wish to call him an *elitist*, he could not help it. That is how he was raised. He did not think in those terms. He was who he was, and he had a drive to spread what is now known as the *Word*—the subtitle of this book: *A Man Driven by the Word*. That described him perfectly.

He did not always know what he was speaking about. He had his own ideas, but he did not know deeply what the whole Kingdom of God meant either. Many times the crowd was disrespectful. I can remember those times myself. Whenever you are going to put yourself out there as a public speaker, there will be those people who will not respect what you are attempting to say, to teach, to do. Many times they are coming from their own ego, for there will be something within themselves where they need the attention drawn to themselves; so they will heckle someone else and in that way they have everyone's eyes upon them—all the attention upon them.

Paul did not let the jeers get to him while speaking. Now, it looked as if he was not bothered by the remarks thrown at him, but he was. It is only human nature to be bothered. It does affect you emotionally so that you start to question yourself. If the heckling is loud enough and frequent enough and if you have any doubts about yourself, this will cause a great emotional disturbance for you.

Now, as I started to speak, this book has the purpose of undermining some of the belief systems that people hold for Christianity. One of the belief systems was how they put Paul up on a pedestal and praised him and prayed to him for miracles. They gave him a god-like status. Since Paul never had this type of attention growing up, it felt good to him. People were recognizing him. It fed him; it gave to him. At the same time, he was conscious of the fact that he was teaching a new philosophy to the people. That is why he repeated his themes so many times.

We have other people we could bring forth. We do not think it is necessary. We think the book stands by itself—a little booklet full of information and full of energy. Therefore, Readers, we believe that we will bring this to a conclusion. It is time to let it go forth. Now the author will have things she needs to write still, but on the whole, it is finished. The following will be the *Closing Statement*.

I did not hate Paul; I was angry with him, but I also forgive him. That lifetime was so many eons ago. It is time to let it go.

This book will serve as a little pebble thrown into the stream of Christianity—a little pebble that could eventually change the flow of the energy. Religion will change, people; it must change, because the concept of **religion is man-made**. It was men who took the teachings and made a religion out of it. The Laws of Moses were made into a religion. All of the religions were made by man, distorted then through the generations, each sect putting its different spin on it. I cannot blame one sect over another particularly, for all religions need revising. All religions are not completely truthful.

I am known as *Jesus the Christ*, but you do not know me. Most of you do not even know where I came from. Most of you will be shocked to know I am Galactic. I came from different planets as most of you have, but people will not accept that. We are coming into the Christmas holidays (2009). People want me lying in a manger; they want me to have been born on the 25th of December. That is a myth, a beautiful and endearing myth, people, but it is a myth. I am not that person. I am vaster than that. (*Yeshua was born in April.*)

I pledged that I would come to Earth and help humanity to raise its consciousness. Whether I have succeeded or not, I do not know. That is what Paul was attempting to do whether he knew it or not. Each soul has a purpose when he comes to the planet; or we will say *it*, for It can be androgynous. Mother Earth is a beautiful Being, so creative, one of the most creative planets in the Universe. The wealth of her species is magnificent.

Our dearest Readers, I am concluding this book and I give my greatest appreciation to this author and to Paul of Tarsus for allowing us to dissect his lifetime, to allow his linen to be aired to the public. Open your hearts, Readers, and know that Paulus of Tarsus did well in that lifetime. He dedicated his life to this service to me and to the Father. He will come in to say a few words for the Closing Statement and then the book is finished.

I AM Yeshua and I salute all of you.

(*Thank you Yeshua*) You are welcome dearest one. We thought it was time to draw the book to a close. Paulus will now step forward.

*But rise and stand upon thy feet, for I have appeared unto thee for this purpose, to make thee a minister and a witness both of these things which thou hast seen, and of those things the which I will appear unto thee (Acts 26:16)*

*Delivering thee from the people and from the Gentiles, unto whom I now send thee (17).*

*To open their eyes and to turn them from darkness to light, and from the power of Satan unto God that they may receive forgiveness of sins and inheritance among them which are sanctified by faith that is in me (18).*

Hello Readers, **I AM Paulus**. You have read my words and have read others' remembrances of me. It was a difficult lifetime. I would not recommend it to any of you. You know, when you are in your lifetime, what can you do but live it! So I lived it to my utmost. I was beaten down and got up again; beaten down and got up again. I was thrown in prison, got out and was up and running again.

I felt blessed, for I was carrying the Lord's Words. I felt very blessed.

Thank you dear Readers, for reading about me and my life. I hope that this will awaken you so that when you look at the other Biblical characters, the Saints and the Prophets, you will start seeing them as human beings. Take off your rose-colored glasses; observe their mistakes. Observe how they were not always in their body. Observe how many times they neglected their body. Discern whether they always spoke truth for all or not. Or were they just following their own ideological feelings? Thank you, Readers; I am honored to have been speaking with you. I AM Paulus of Tarsus.

*Finally, brethren, whatsoever things are true, whatsoever things are honest, whatsoever things are just, whatsoever things are pure, whatsoever things are lovely, whatsoever things are of good report, if there be any virtue, if there be any praise, think on these things (Ph 4:8.)*

Dear one this is your little book. It is up to you now to bring it to a close. 'Til we meet again, dear one, I AM Yeshua. *(Thank you. 11-24-09, revised 3-10-12.)*

# EPILOGUE

Well, dear Readers, it has been a short ride, but I hope it has been full of wonders for you—such revelations from our friend Paulus, et al. Many artists throughout the centuries have painted him with their own renditions—one being **Rembrandt** who would use a **self-portrait** for his painting of Paul. There is a plethora of paintings on the Internet, but I did not find one that I felt was the closest to what Paul might have looked like. Hence, I had to give up that idea and go with Michelangelo's beautiful painting that bears no resemblance to Paul, I am sure, is probably too busy a painting for a cover of a book, but it was legally free and clear.

I had a past life dream where I was a Cardinal in the Vatican. I had taken off my red robe and laid it in this large old-fashioned trunk, muttering, *it is too cold in here*, referring to the atmosphere of the Vatican and not the climate of Rome. I was leaving the Vatican. I believe many of us have had past-life dreams of being a priest or a nun. I have had three lives as a village priest and one as a nun working in a leper colony, never catching the disease. I believe souls are researching and experiencing Catholic theology, hoping to make some difference in that distorted religion, hoping to restore correctly some of Yehsua's teachings.

manwww.newworldencyclopedia.org/entry/Paul_of_Tarsus is a website worth perusing. It prints out 18 pages of facts (*or fiction*) that may interest the reader.

I have referenced all Biblical quotes using the King James Version. My Bible is from the Royal Publishers, Inc. (1971).

Although I have read the Bible from cover to cover at least twice, I do not feel that I am a student or an authority on the Bible, let alone on Paul's life. (*Just because you lived then also does not mean you remember any of it!*) I have a tremendous drive. Whenever I set out upon a particular endeavor, I see it to its end—through blood, sweat, and tears I get it done. We are all Divine Beings millions of years old. Who knows what or where we have left our foot-prints in the sand? History makes claims that Jesus was the *founder* and Paul was the *maker* of Christianity. It is for you to decide.

Therefore, dear Readers, I bring this book to a close with this quote: *For I am the least of the apostles, that am not meet to be called an apostle, because I persecuted the church of God. (1Co 15:9)*

*But by the grace of God I am what I am: and his grace which was bestowed upon me was not in vain; but I labored more abundantly than they all; yet not I, but the grace of God which was with me. (10).*

*Therefore, whether it were I or they, so we preached, and so ye believed. (11).*

Blessings to you dear Readers, 'til we meet again in 2012, I AM Chako.

# ABOUT THE AUTHOR

Verling CHAKO Priest, PhD was born in Juneau, Alaska, hence her name of Cheechako, shortened to just Chako by her mother, a medical doctor, and her father, an Orthodontist. Chako was raised in Napa, CA. She attended the University of California at Berkeley where she met her future husband. Upon their marriage and after his training as a Navy pilot, they settled into the military way of life. They lived twelve years outside of the United States Mainland in various places, which included Hawaii, Viet Nam, Australia, and Greece. Little did she know that these exotic lands and peoples were preparing her for her spiritual awakening years hence?

After her husband's retirement from the Navy, they resettled in Napa, California. It was during this time that she returned to school at Berkeley, transferred to Sonoma University where she earned her first two degrees in Psychology. Chako then entered the doctoral program at the Institute of Transpersonal Psychology (ITP) at Menlo Park, CA, (and now renamed Sofia University) which is located in Palo Alto, CA. She successfully completed that program which consisted of a Master, as well as the Doctorate in Transpersonal Psychology. Ten years and four degrees later she was able to pursue her passion for Metaphysical and New Age Thought—her introduction into the realm of the Spiritual Hierarchy and the Ascended Lords and Masters.

In 1988, Dr. Priest moved to Minnetonka, Minnesota. She co-authored a program called, *Second Time Around* for those with recurring cancer for Methodist Hospital. She, as a volunteer, also facilitated a grief group for Pathways of Minneapolis, and had a private practice.

She studied with a spiritual group in Minnetonka led by Donna Taylor and the Teacher, a group of 5 highly developed entities channeled by Donna. The group traveled extensively all over the world working with the energy grids of the planet and regaining parts of their energies that were still in sacred areas waiting to be reclaimed by them, the owners. They climbed in and out of the pyramids in Egypt, tromped through the Amazon forest in Venezuela, rode camels at Sinai, and climbed the Mountain. Hiked the paths at Qumran, trod the ancient roadways in Petra, Jordan, and walked where the Master Yeshua walked in Israel.

The time came, November 1999, when Chako was guided to move to Arizona—her next phase of growth. This is where she found her beloved Masters, who in reality had always been with her. They were **all** ready for her next phase, bringing into the physical several books—mind-provoking books, telepathically received by her, from these highly evolved, beautiful, loving Beings. Each book stretches her capabilities, as well as her belief systems. Nevertheless, it is a challenge she gladly embraces.

It is now November 2009.* She just has finished writing her eighth book. She has been told that a ninth book may be started in April 2010. There is no hint as to the theme. (*The Goddess Returns to Earth, 2010*)

*Comments:*

*AZCHAKO@AOL.COM*

*It is now March 10, 2012 and I am thoroughly intent on revising this previous edition. When I told Jeshua what I was up to he replied, *I support you in that decision and as you say, it will do a service just having more truth brought into it.*

Saint Germain once told me that the Masters ride the waves of the library of our mind and channel their words from that.

Distortions can and do happen, especially if the vehicle's bias or childhood programming and/or ego slips in and out during a session. Most people channel from 45 minutes to 90 minutes (the duration of a tape). During that time, the channel is in a deep, concentrated trance, listening and parroting the Masters' words. At any time the channel may lose his/her concentration, which allows distortion to creep in. It happens to all of us, no exceptions. Therefore, a revised book catches most of those "bloopers" and brings forth an even higher percentage of truth.

Jeshua has long expressed a desire to bring forth a book for humanity. It is in the works—*Jesus: My Beloved Connection to Humanity and the Sea*—early summer 2012.